PANDEMONIUM

AAROOSH KHAN

PANDEMONIUM

ISBN: —

First Printing, November 2024.

www.aarooshkhan.com

PANDEMONIUM

TABLE OF CONTENTS

ABOUT THE AUTHOR

Aaroosh Khan is the youngest author in her genre. She's also the first teen author from her city, and one of the youngest in her country, Pakistan. Her debut novel, *The Echoes of Erebus Stygian*, was released June 2024, and is loved as a light-hearted YA Low Fantasy. She's currently working on multiple books, and plans to share them with the world soon! When Aaroosh is not writing—or making Pinterest boards/daydreaming about her characters—she can be found reading books, crocheting, working on her literary magazine, *The Cassiopeia Review,* or managing her small businesses. She is ardent to share her writing, and to connect with readers all over the world.

Find her at @written.by.aaroosh *&* @aaroosh.writes on Instagram, and on her website as well: *www.aarooshkhan.com*!

PANDEMONIUM

DEDICATION:

For my parents, and my sister, Zaynab.

And for everyone who cheered me on when I was nothing but a girl with the dream to become a published author.

I love you all so much.

PANDEMONIUM

PANDEMONIUM

a poetry collection

AAROOSH KHAN

I.

MOTEL ROOM MOTHS

visible cracks in the motel room's unclad, wallpaper-less walls
water drips down the damp ceiling as you rest on the battered mattress
almost lifeless.

cracked, dry lips and a face so pale
even a ghost would be humiliated.

turn to your side, your cheek flattened against the tinged blanket.
curl up into a ball
wallow in pity.

are you really that revolting?
are you really that bad?
coward, foolish, incompetent failure.

PANDEMONIUM

is that really who you are?
who even *are* you?

the question only echoes off the petite motel room's hollow space.

the too-square window lets in a guest
a moth, fluttering across the putrid room
a pang of jealousy burns through your heart; *even a moth is so free and assured.*

you? could *you* handle that?
the room disagrees as its broken lights flicker.

your mouth and throat are like sandpaper
limbs as weak as cardboard
yet your mind is so strong as it continues to insult you.

their ill words rage around you, smothering the air
perhaps disguising themselves as the moth that continues to *flap flap* around the room.

why, my dear, would you ever distrust yourself?
this honey-coated world is
w e a k
you are not.

escape this tomb the mortals have barred you in.

hold your heart so close and follow the moth's exhausted
movements
forget this world like it would forget you
move your cardboard limbs and let your heart work as the moth's
did.

find your redemption
because, my dear
death has not come yet.

you still have a life to live
and a heart to save.

II.

YOUR ILL-STARRED DREAMS

honey-sweet words and the chirping of birds once filled your ears
the sky was once blue and you had no fears.

days passed by, so slow, so warm
there were never signs of any storm.

a blurry dream, passing by so fast
a forgotten memory, one you found at last
tucked away in some corner of your mind
you desperately try to hold on, looking for the light that once shined.

the dream is slipping away
every color is turning to gray
you frantically try to remember and hold on
but it slips away like sand through your fingers

in moments, *it's gone.*

now all that remain are withering blurs
these memories and dreams were only voyagers.

those liquid, calming words
and the dreams where you saw those beautiful, golden birds.
the brazen feeling that hung by

the way the world went twirling and whirling and never let you say
goodbye
it locked you into a dusty, old tomb
the walls closing in moment by moment until there was no
room—

your eyes fly open and everything has gone wild
your clothes are too tight and your hair is too sticky and those
dreams only smiled.

'wretched, wretched, wretched,' you spit out
but you were the one who wanted these ill-starred dreams to stay

PANDEMONIUM

oh, you realize

these aren't those dreams anymore; not those stories you liked to immortalize.

these are merely a mirage of what you've lived in

a ruse by your mind—

a blur of your thoughts—

a reflection of you—

a reflection of your nightmares.

III.

DEAR PERSEPHONE'S DREAMS

she sat and wrote one day

speaking what they would not let her say:

a monochrome life, devoid of any hues

all I feel and see are terrible blues.

once I felt something silly called hope

now everything is slipping away as if coated with soap.

the mundane was supposed to be my muse

but now everything is mundane and there is no use.

no matter how many words I angrily etch down

the misty wind and dull grass continue to ruin my nightgown.

time is slipping away

PANDEMONIUM

their hopes and dreams have already been crumbled in a stupid ashtray.

I must hold on to my vivid and tranquil world
where dreams and stories exultantly unfurled
where the wind used to be so sickly sweet
where the flowers once bloomed and the grass used to crunch under my feet.

now everything is so horribly bland
was this really what we called our motherland?

shrill screams echo at night
no one reacts, they've lost their fright.

the world has turned into a rotting tomb
this is our end, this is our doom.

someone violently shakes me back to reality—
'oh, Persephone! quit this profanity!'

Persephone had been dreaming again
'forget about that world!' the lady barks, snapping Persephone's
pen
breaking it to pieces, and then—
fuming anger spills out of the girl
though she sits silently, letting her emotions uncurl.

'dreams and stories are meant to be forgotten,' they say
but dear Persephone will clutch on tight to them, no matter what
price she has to pay.

IV.

DEAR PERSEPHONE'S REBELLION

It's 3:56 am and Persephone remains awake
eyes stinging from sleep but she can't stop scrawling down

words that heaved her heart down and bellowed in her mind
words that were atrocious, sinister thoughts, even.

they'd try to stop her for this careless behavior
but the shackles around Persephone's mind only tattered onto the ground.

dear Persephone does not let go of her world
she does not give in to this new reality
Persephone feels her blood rush through her, hot and cold
Persephone feels alive, unlike those who rule her.

immoral, vile, foolish people
stealing her dreams and giving her woes.

even though there were arrows striking her chest

Persephone never stopped etching her words down

the hatred she felt for this world
the unfair change that had occurred
the earth seemed to careen towards its peril
and Persephone wasn't going to forget when everything was better.

she was a girl who dreamed
a girl who saved her heart—chained and kept away in those wooden trunks in her grand room.

even though she was meant to forget
Persephone won't let go, not yet.

clutching her dreams tight to her hollow chest
stories that felt like liquid, running through her blood
magic that made the gray sky glitter every day
and melodies that muffled the screams around town.

Persephone lives a better life than they know.

V.

WATCH & FEEL

clammy, murky, briny smells

steps hastening, and the wind fails

hand in pocket, the other is freezing cold

cough

toss away your smoking cigarette

agile moonlight, dazed vision

thin alley—bony and scrawny like your courage

you trip over something brawny; *is that a body?*

no, no, it isn't, only your imprudent head's ruses

hair sticking to your perspiring face

breathing shallow, and your blood indolently circulates.

your heart once thrived

and now, it barely survived.

take a glance back

be delirious once again

does the figure following you hold a knife? *Is it death?*

wet gravel champs under your feet

the wind whispers, *'again we shall meet.'*

everything has appallingly ceased

your clothes are tacky, there's sweat all over your body

hotness blisters your skin and then—

the wind has deceived you

your feet have stopped

the moon twinkles derisively

the stiletto is at your throat.

lose yourself

death has come

don't run away.

AAROOSH KHAN

'it'll be all right,' says the wind
grasp the figure's cold, cold hand
pull away the knife, as you tremble
blood oozes out of your gaunt finger.

'this is only the beginning,' the figure mouths.

watch the fellow disperse like writings splashed away by the tide
watch yourself stagger when you see your hand unscathed
watch the world spin and deadbolt you away
watch the wind return, and watch your heart defy
watch the sky go black
watch the moon turn to cinders, and your vision starts to lack—

now feel
feel the moist gravel scrape your face as you fall
feel its gritty, metallic taste as you try to crawl
feel your eyes flutter close
feel your limbs give out
feel your feet go numb

PANDEMONIUM

feel yourself thaw like beeswax and then—

feel someone trip over your arm.

'memento mori,' they said

now death has finally come

dressed in silver; hands so cold

study its face—it's not death, *it's you.*

death has still not arrived

it was only your mind playing tricks on you.

the knife is still freezing against your throat

the gravel is still in your mouth

damp.

feel yourself lose the world

feel yourself lose yourself

feel yourself go insane—

and watch yourself fall.

VI.

VOID

blurred vision, havoc wreaks

the ghosts around you have suddenly

vanished.

your legs, boneless, scrawny things, give out as you tumble

through a void

where did your heart and mind go?

they've done what they always do

they've *betrayed* you.

your eyes flutter close so weakly

the pandemonium around you seems to mock your bravery.

where have your heart and mind gone? something whispers in your

ear

voice so velvety, as soft as a blanket on a freezing night

'have you tried running away again?'

you try to nod all so strongly

your bones crumble to the ground like limestone

you find yourself waiting for the end.

does the end come for those who wish for it?

'It doesn't,' the wind rasps. *'go to sleep, my dear.'*

listen to the treacherous wind

let your eyes flutter close

become one with the void.

body melting like glaciers joining the sea

heavy eyelids

your vision is gone

body boneless

your skin is peeling off

a stinging pain in your hollow chest

your heart has finally returned

but it is only rabid.

'go to sleep, my dear,' the wind repeats, *'this might be the end.'*

close your eyes

solid metal fills your mouth

lead seeps through your blood.

this is your end

this is your redemption

this is your escape

this is your void.

VII.

I WONDER WHY WE LOST OUR BLISS

gazing at the kite-filled sky with awe as the sunlight pierces
through my eyes
sitting cross-legged on the colorful *chaarpayi*
peeling those oranges with my bare hands
that excitement when our favorite shows used to play on the old
TV.

the sweet gulaab jamun
the sweet *rasgullay*
life was so simple
a mirage of love, care, and pleasure.

the soaring kites that once filled the sky
are now gone, I wonder why.

the *chaarpayi* once went for repair

it never returned, I only stared at its vacant space.

those shows were never again on the television
and the sweets never excited us
everything was lost, and I wonder why—

I wonder why we let go of happiness.
I wonder why we lost our bliss.

VIII.

THE LIBRARY OF LOST MINDS

click, clack

doors unlocked as tears dropped to the grounds
glittering diamonds
a treasure for the kingdom
a blanket of grief.

'where are they headed?' they whispered
'to the library of lost minds,' answers the moth that flutters by their ears.

the library that holds your darkest secrets
your regrets
your failures
and the dreams you abandoned.

the humans that were lost

the lies that were concealed

the honey-suckled truths that were too bitter

swallow

they sting your throat.

crippling books breathe on the abandoned shelves—

—forsaken.

hungry for human touch

with teeth that would tear down your ribs and heart.

the little girl's dream to become a medic remained a dream

buried

gone

forgotten

just a dream.

the young boy's wish to make the world a better place was only

suppressed

he became a tyrant—a ruler who only destroyed the world

irony breaks his bones as they crumble with age.

what about you?

where do your dreams lie?

what reality do you live in?

'one not of the library of lost minds,' hopes the wind

for they are lost, gone, forgotten—

dead.

IX.

CRIMSON EYES THAT STARED INTO YOURS

which of these faces is yours?

shattered mirrors are all that surround you.

each crack is a story

eyes darting everywhere

fingers tracing each slit

a porcelain-skinned face stares back at you

its smile cutting through its cheeks

is that you?

do you recognize yourself?

or do you look for the blood-stricken, cracked appearance first?

crimson eyes staring into yours

hair so long and silky.

you reach out to touch

PANDEMONIUM

crack

shattered glass pricks your fingers.

roses have thorns

and the shiniest of glass could slit your throat, too.

your skin is cracked

hollow cheeks

scarlet eyes

unknown.

click, clack

they're watching

they're watching every step you take and every image you paint with your blood.

can you recognize yourself amid faces you wish were yours?

or will you forget yourself for beauty that will rot you from inside out?

like worm-infested, rotten lemons

that crave your love

but they're thrown away

forgotten.

what does that teach you?

if you wish to be remembered, you must remember yourself.

X.

THE FIRE HAS TURNED TO ASH

a lit cigarette between your index and middle finger
the smoke stings your throat
yet you can't stay away from it.

the wind howls in your ears
the window panes rattle
uneasy.

forget about the cigarette
dip it in your ashtray
the smoke dissipates in seconds as the fire turns to ash
perhaps like you.

humans, mortals, living beings
all of their dreams?
gone.

turned to ash.

stare out the dirty window

as the moon winks

where did humanity go?

these men and women boast their power

their goals

their lies are nothing but accomplishments.

'what are humans without humanity?' you ask the moon

it only twinkles silently before it speaks.

'what about you? where did your dreams and kindness go?' the

moon asks

'in the ashtray,' you answer

dipped away, turned to dust

nothing but mere residue

vanished.

all of us have lost our sympathy

PANDEMONIUM

our hearts

our minds

shackled.

humanity is gone

so are humans

all that remain are mortals who are too cruel to each other.

'scoundrels,' the moon laughs.

the fire has turned to ash

and the moon, admired by the beasts, even

is nothing but a rock that steals from the sun.

pandemonium is all that surrounds us.

the liars are the truthful

the truthful are the liars

and perhaps, you are the reason why.

'ignorant mortal,' says the moon as your eyes shut

slowly

sickly

farewell.

XI.

WHERE DID HOME GO?

jagged, honey-painted, crumbling walls

pale, hollow, cold face.

where are you?

floating through a void where you

do not belong

do not understand

do not feel

do not live.

what is this foreign, mundane place?

home?

can't be, the wind hums in your ears.

concrete walls surround you

cracks running through them

perhaps mirroring you.

one tiny window
there's no daylight coming through.

the carpets sting your feet as you walk
smudging blood along the perfect linoleum flooring.

lights flicker every passing moment
the hallways are thin
empty
dark
closing in every second
like an alley with Death hiding in it.

this isn't home.

it isn't the place where you used to sit on the colorful chaarpayi
peeling oranges with your bare hands.

PANDEMONIUM

this isn't the place where you felt the warmth of *daadi's* hand-sewn *razai.*

this isn't the place where you waited for the rain to drench you.

this isn't the place where gray clouds meant you'd get *ammi*'s *pakoray.*

this isn't the place where even the mud felt yours.

this isn't the place you used to call home.
ghar.
mera ghar.

this isn't the place you want to return to every day
this isn't *home.*
'where did home go?' you ask
'you left it behind,' the wind answers
home's gone.
locked away.

AAROOSH KHAN

dust covers the floors you used to play on
dust covers the *jhoola* you fought your *bhai* for
dust covers your dreams and life and your home.

it's gone.

locked up
damp
cold
hollow
like you
home's gone,
and only living between these cold, cemented walls made you
realize.

PANDEMONIUM

ACKNOWLEDGEMENTS

I published my debut novel in June '24, and never expected to come up with a poetry book the same year, too, but here we are. It's somewhat unbelievable sometimes—being the youngest author in my genre and actually achieving what I dreamt of as a child.

The first people to thank are my parents, for helping me fulfill this dream of becoming an author, and for being there for every step of the journey. I love you both so much—and I don't know what I'd do without you.

I'd also like to thank my friends—Fatima, Samavia, Zynab, and a few others, for enduring long rant sessions and helping me with my cover design problems (this one's for you Sam).

Major appreciation goes to my beta-readers as well: Menal (always here for me), Shanaya (thank you for all the help), Barisi (the best).

I'm very grateful for every person who has been a part of this journey; whether it be my writing friends, or supporters online and offline, I love you all so much!

Lastly, I hope that this poetry book/chapbook touches your heart, and that it inspires other young writers like me to achieve their dreams, too.

Here's to more books to come!

AAROOSH KHAN

www.ingramcontent.com/pod-product-compliance
Lightning Source LLC
LaVergne TN
LVHW041253150826
845673LV00008B/2569

* 9 7 8 9 6 9 2 2 6 9 8 5 8 *